The ultimate ski maint~~

b~

Learn to love your s~ ~
spend maximum tir~ ~g ~~~~ly and
effortlessly on the slopes this winter:

The Ultimate Ski Maintenance Book gives simple step-by-step instructions on everything you need to know in order to take care of your skis from home.

The book is packed full of photos illustrating each procedure in an easy-to-follow manner that absolutely anyone – youngster to adult, novice to professional – will benefit.

From basic safety check to home waxing and through to damage repair, The Ultimate Ski Maintenance Book has you covered.

Acknowledgments

The author's thanks to those who contributed time and resources towards the effort of writing the book.

Copyright © 2015 by Peter Ballin

All rights reserved. No part of this publication may be reproduced, distributed, or transmitted in any form or by any means, including photocopying, recording, or other electronic or mechanical methods, without the prior written permission of the publisher, except in the case of brief quotations embodied in critical reviews and certain other noncommercial uses permitted by copyright law.

tutorial Illustrations Copyright © 2015 Ben Raynor

Warning

This book is designed to provide information on ski maintenance only. This information is provided and sold with the knowledge that the publisher and author do not offer any legal or other professional advice. In the case of a need for any such expertise consult with the appropriate professional. This book does not contain all information available on the subject. This book has not been created to be specific to any individual's or organizations' situation or needs. Every effort has been made to make this book as accurate as possible. However, there may be typographical and or content errors. Therefore, this book should serve only as a general guide and not as the ultimate source of subject information. This book contains information that might be dated and is intended only to educate and entertain. The author and publisher shall have no liability or responsibility to any person or entity regarding any loss or damage incurred, or alleged to have incurred, directly or indirectly, by the information contained in this book. You hereby agree to be bound by this disclaimer or you may return this book within the guarantee time period for a full refund

About the author

The author of this book Peter Ballin has a wide range of experiences and interests, from skiing fresh powder in the French Alps to being an accomplished mountain bike racer and world cup mechanic. When he's not in the mountains he can often be found taking on new challenges like swimming across lake Geneva or hitch hiking across America with his surfboard.

His idea for this book was born from many winters working as a ski technician, where he taught fellow ski enthusiasts how to service their own equipment. Once he saw how much people enjoyed being able to service their own skis, he decided to write this book to help more people look after their skis.

Contents

A GUIDE TO BUYING SKI TOOLS

Ski vices 10
DIY ski vice 11
Ski Irons. 12
Home/Travel irons 13
Plexi-glass scrapers (plastic) 14
Metal scrapers 15
Gummy stones. 16
Edge files 20
Panzer body files. 22
File guides/holders 23
Sidewall cutters. 26
Brushes. 27

EDGES: SHARPENING, BEVELING, AND TUNING

What is bevelling?. 34
Understanding base edge beveling. 35
Understanding side edge beveling 38
How to sharpen and tune edges 40
Detuning edges 51

BASE REPAIRS, FIXING SCRAPES, HOLES AND DINGS

What is P-tex? 57
What is metal grip? 58
How to repair holes in your base 59

WAXES AND WAXING

Why do skis need waxing?. 68
What are temperature waxes?. 70
Which type of wax should I use? 72
How to wax skis. 74
How often do I need to wax my skis?. 84
Do I need to wax new skis? 86

SUMMER LOVING

How to protect your skis for the summer 90

A guide to buying ski tools

This section of the book describes various specialist ski tools and their use. You may not need to use all the tools, but it will make you a better ski tuner if you use the right tool for the job at hand.

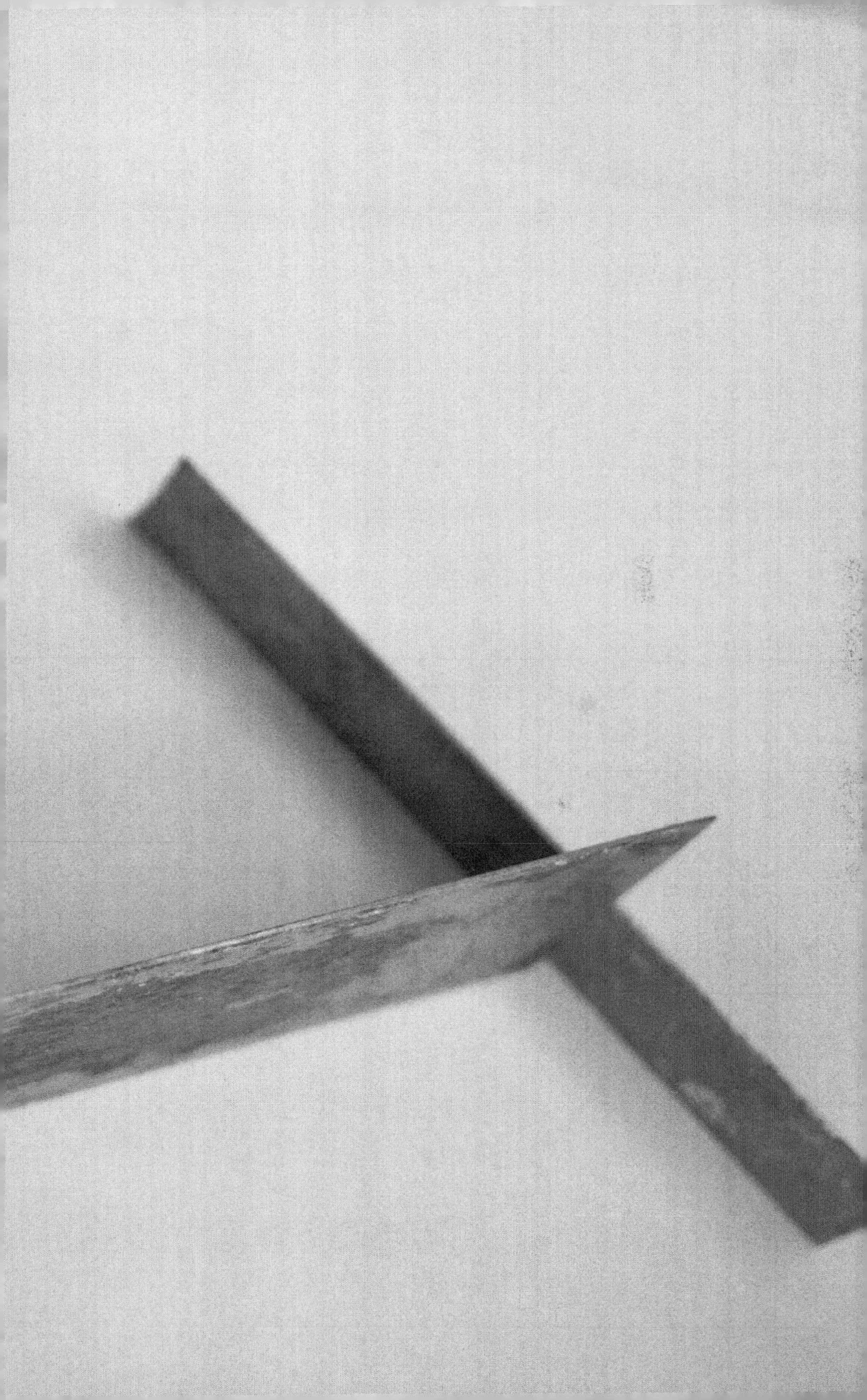

Ski vices

A ski vice helps to support the skis while they are being worked on; the skis can normally be mounted flat for base work or upright for edge work. If you're serious about servicing your skis, then a good ski vice is a worthwhile investment.

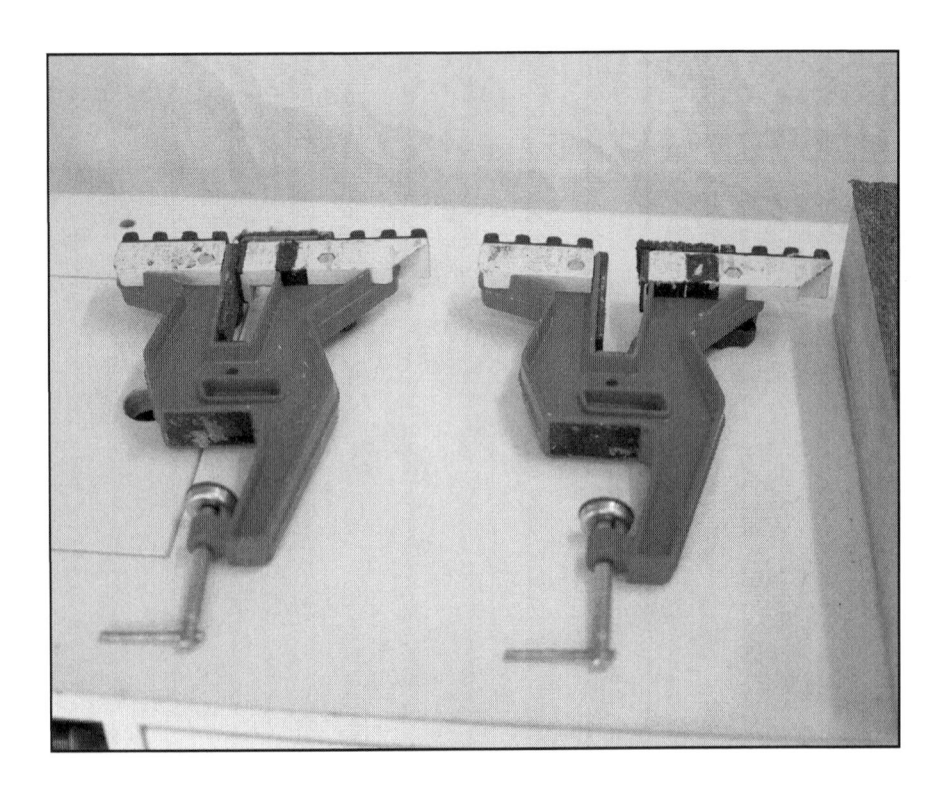

DIY ski vice

For most jobs, you can rest your skis on two blocks of wood. This will provide a sufficient working area, and save you money.

Ski Irons

Specialist ski irons are effective because you can adjust the temperature to ensure they don't burn the wax, and they also have a wide, flat area to help give a nice, even spread of wax.

Home/Travel irons

If you're on a budget, you can get a travel iron for around £3 ($5) which should do the job perfectly well—just make sure not to use the steam setting and, as with all irons, keep it moving so you don't burn the base.

Remember: don't use your mum's home iron, because it will leave marks on clothes after you have used it with wax.

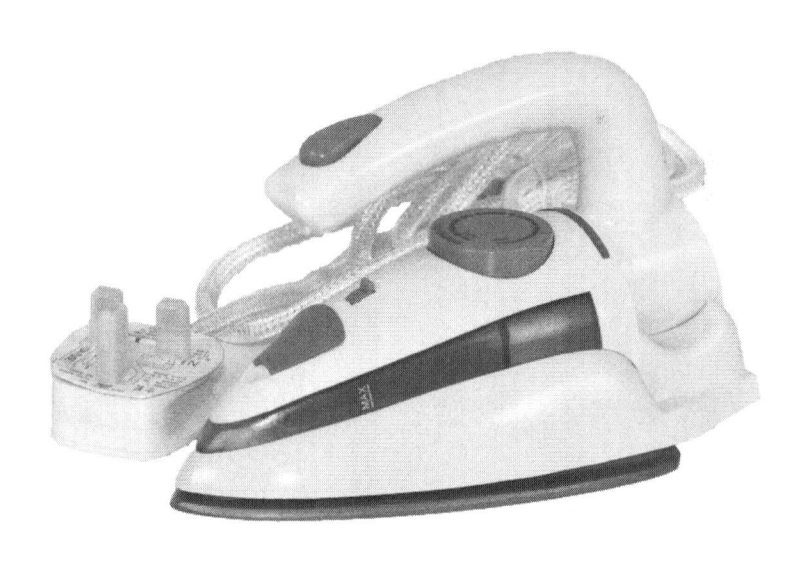

Plexi-glass scrapers (plastic)

Plastic scrapers are used to remove the majority of the wax after it has been ironed on. They are normally made from Plexi-glass, and vary from 3–5mm in thickness. It's important to keep the scraper sharp using a file or a scraper sharpener, which sharpens the scraper to 90°. On the side of most scrapers, you will notice a small notch: this is for removing wax from the edges.

Metal scrapers

Metal scrapers are best used to push hot P-tex into fills so that it bonds well, and can then be carefully used to gently scrape away the excess P-tex. When scraping with a metal scraper, apply medium pressure and use gentle scrapes to avoid causing any damage. You can use a metal scraper to scrape wax, but this is not recommended because it's easy to slip and take a gouge out of your base.

Gummy stones

A gummy stone is used to get rid of micro-burrs after you have sharpened your edges. They can also be used to help clean up the edges before you sharpen them. Gummy stones usually come in four different grades:

- Grey: If you only have the money for one gummy stone, get this one: it's the softest, and can be used for both removing micro-burrs and detuning the tips and tails (see: Detuning).

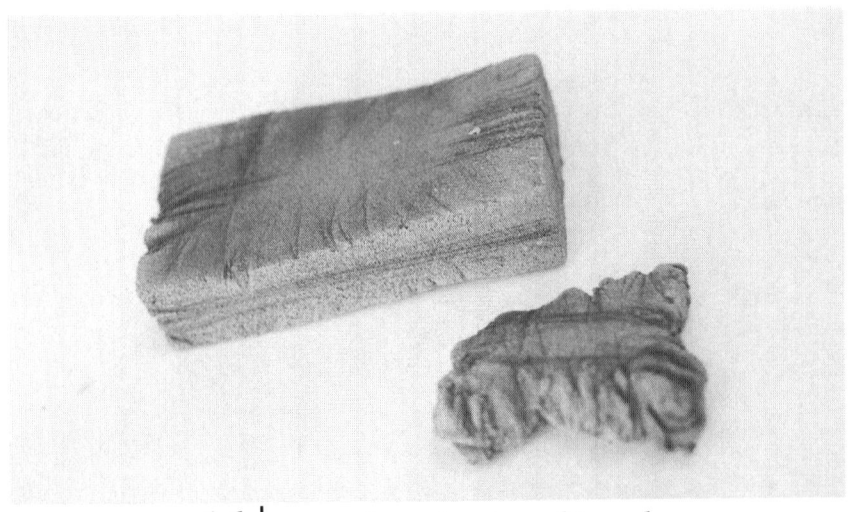

- Red: Can also be used to help remove micro-burrs, and is good for polishing after filing.

- White : This is a medium stone that is used to remove tough burrs and deformities.

- Blue: This is an extra hard stone which is used on very heavily burred edges.

Ceramic stones

After filing and applying a diamond stone, ceramic stones are used to give an unbeatable polished finish. They come in two different types: hard and soft. The most common are soft stones, which are often used by ski racers to polish and refine a freshly cut bevel. Hard stones are used to remove striations, helping to prolong the sharpness of the edge.

Diamond stones

Diamond stones are used like files, and can also be used with a file guide. The advantage of diamond stones is that they come in a wide range of coarseness grades, with each grade suited to a specific purpose from de-burring to polishing. The coarseness ranges from 100–1000 grit (the lower the number, the coarser the stone). For example, 100-grit diamond stones are extremely coarse, and would normally be used for de-burring major deformities such as rock hits. At the other end of the spectrum, 1000-grit stones are regularly used by ski racers to give an accurate, honed, and polished finish.

Edge files

Files are generally used to cut bevels and sharpen edges. The main factor to consider with files is the number of teeth per centimeter (TPC), which determines how coarse the file is and therefore at which stage in the process it should be used. The fewer TPC, the more aggressive the file, and thus the more material will be removed. Files with a higher TCP value remove less material, and are generally used for polishing. The three main types of file are:

Bastard or Traditional (First-cut file)
This is the most aggressive file, with around 10-12 TPC. This is ideal for removing deep rock damage, cutting a new bevel, or detuning edges for park skiing. If you're looking for one file to do it all, the bastard is not suitable, because it leaves serrations that need to be followed up with a smoother file.

Second-cut file

Second-cut files have around 16 TPC. These smaller teeth do not remove enough material to change the bevel, but are normally used after the first cut to refile and improve the sharpness. Because of this, they are good all-round files, which make them great for a ski tuner looking for a good all-round file.

Fine cut (finishing-cut file)

Fine cut files have around 20 TPC. These fine teeth are designed to remove any notches left by the bastard or second-cut files. Although these can be practical files to own, diamond stones will normally give a better finish.

Panzer body files

These extremely aggressive files are mainly used for removing excess base material. They are very useful for removing excess P-tex after a fill, but can also be used to flatten bases or sharpen scrapers.

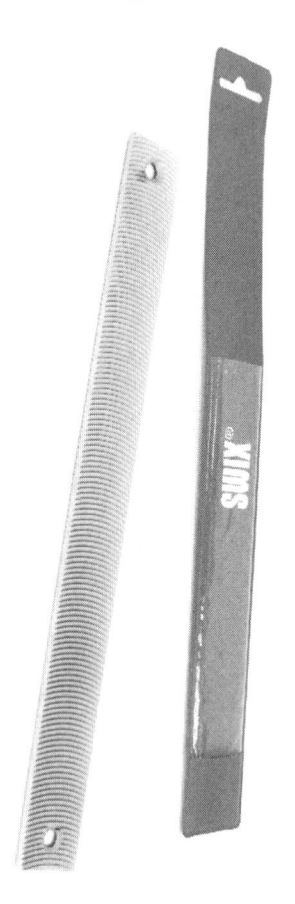

File guides/holders

File guides are designed to work with files or stones to accurately cut the desired bevel. They are a must-have for anyone wanting to sharpen or bevel their edges.

They come in a multitude of colors and sizes. Generally, metal guides are harder wearing and less flexible, which will give a more precise and consistent cut. There are two main types of file guide: multiple angle guides and single angle guides.

Multiple angle guides

Multiple angle guides are an ideal tool for people who want a guide that does it all. Depending on budget, they may be made of either metal or plastic. The limiting factor with multiple angle guides is that they normally hold files or stones up to a maximum of 40 mm in width, which makes them incompatible with many stones and files that give an enhanced finish.

Single angle guides

Single angle file guides give the most accurate finish possible, and hence are used by professional ski tuners across the world. One of the best features of single angle guides is that they are normally compatible with all files and stones, which enables you to use them for every stage, giving the best possible finish. Single angle guides are normally sold in 1° increments from 83–90° for the side edge and 0.25° increments from 0.5–1.5° for the base edge.

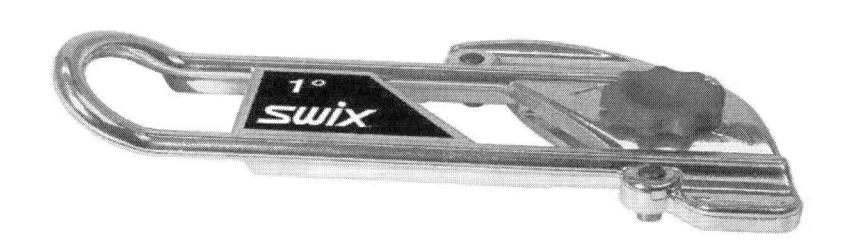

Sidewall cutters

As your skis are sharpened or beveled, they lose material. Eventually, the sidewall will protrude, restricting the ability to bevel or sharpen the edge. A sidewall cutting tool allows you to shave off the protruding sidewall at 90° to the base edge, allowing the desired bevel to be cut. Sidewall cutters are especially useful with skis that use a bevel of 4° or more, such as giant slalom skis.

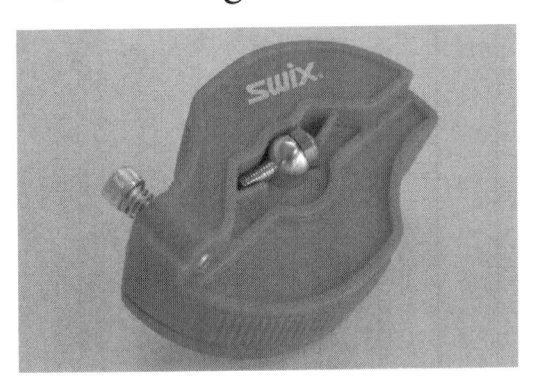

Top tip: it's important to take your time cutting the sidewall, removing only thin layers at a time. This reduces the risk of digging out chunks. Remember to finish the job with some 220-grit silicon carbide sand paper, and then polish off with some 400-grit silicon carbide sand paper.

Brushes

Metal brushes (Pre-wax)

Metal brushes are used to clean the base of oxidants, dirt, or other imperfections before waxing. They also help restore the structure of the base, which will improve wax absorption and result in a better finish. Pre-wax brushes usually have either steel, copper, or bronze bristles. Steel brushes do a better job of cleaning the base, whereas softer copper and bronze bushes are more versatile and can be used as post-waxing brushes to reduce the amount of brushing.

Nylon brushes (post-wax)

Nylon brushes are used after scraping to remove any remaining wax. They come in three different types: a stiff black bristled brush, a medium white bristled brush, and a soft blue bristled brush. For most recreational skiers, a white bristled brush will be more than adequate. The more advanced ski tuner will start with a black brush, and work their way through to the blue brush to remove as much wax as possible, thus providing the maximum amount of slide.

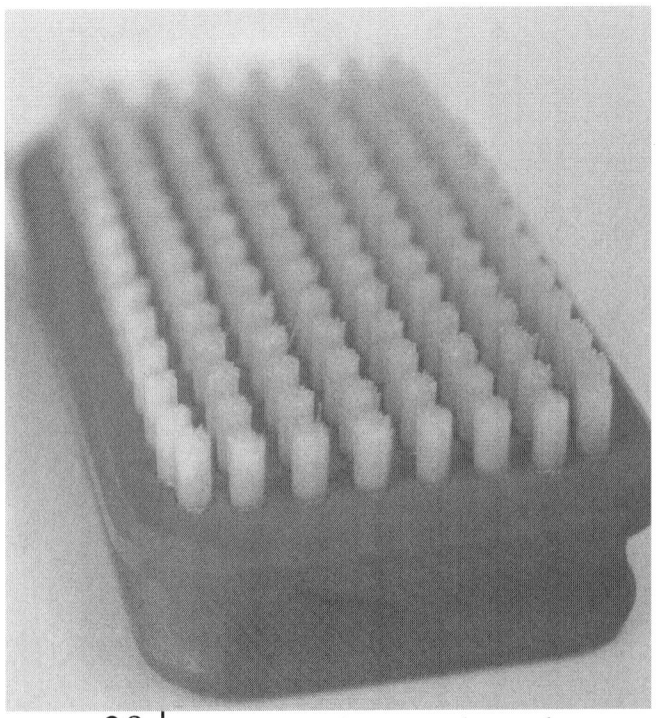

Natural fiber brushes (race wax)

Brushes made of natural fiber (such as horse hair or wild boar hair) are used to apply pure fluorocarbon race waxes. It is very important that natural fiber bushes are only used for fluorocarbon waxes; otherwise, contamination will reduce the effectiveness of the wax.

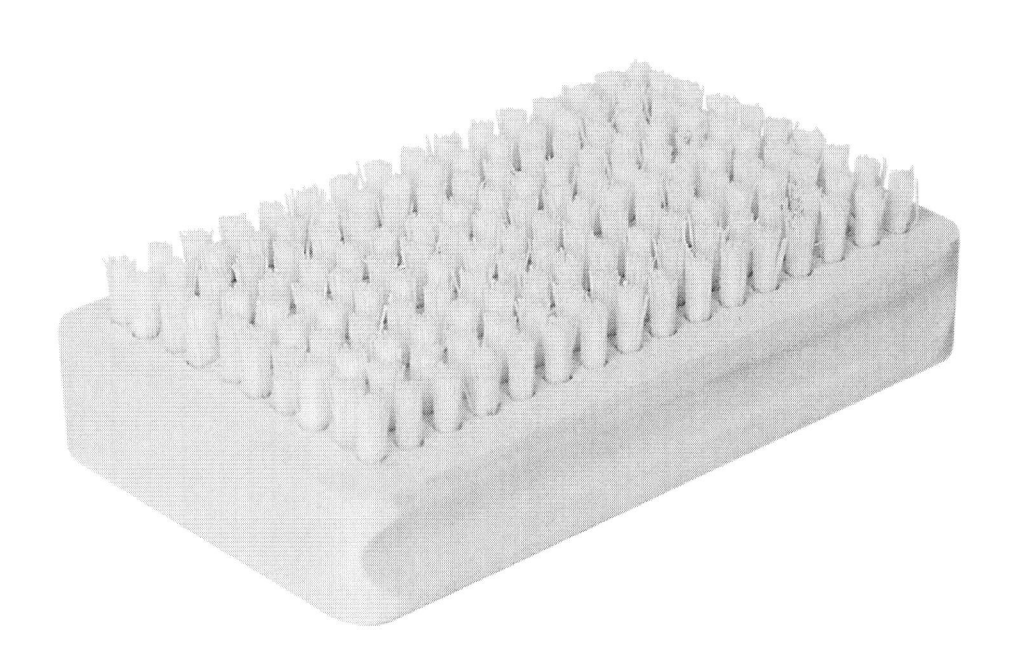

Roto-brushes (post-wax)

Rotor brushes attach to a standard drill, and come in the same variations as standard hand brushes. The main advantage over hand brushes is speed, which can be useful when tuning a large number of skis.

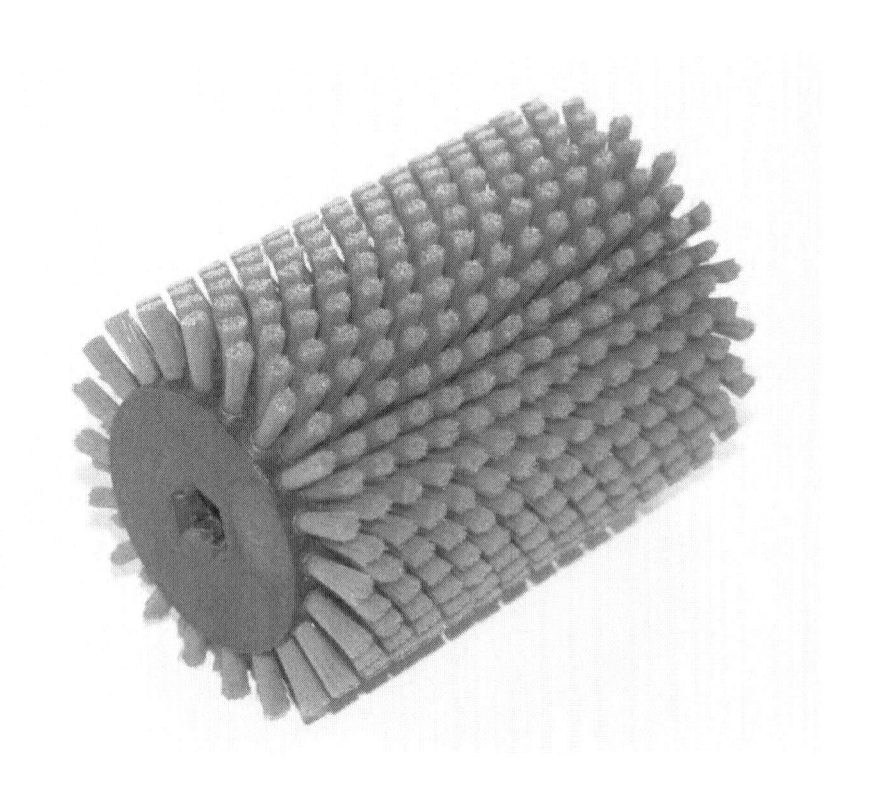

Corks (racing)

Corks are used to apply fluorocarbon race waxes. The friction from the cork melts the fluoros into the base. Most ski racers will use a cork buff to rub in fluorocarbon wax right before a race run.

Edges: Sharpening, beveling, and tuning

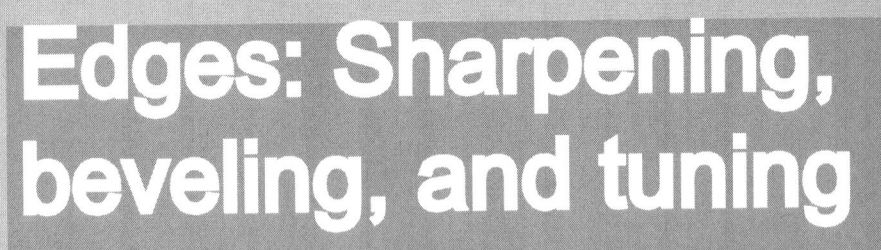

This section of the book explains how to sharpen and tune ski edges. Having the edges set correctly for the ski discipline and snow condition can make the skis perform their best.

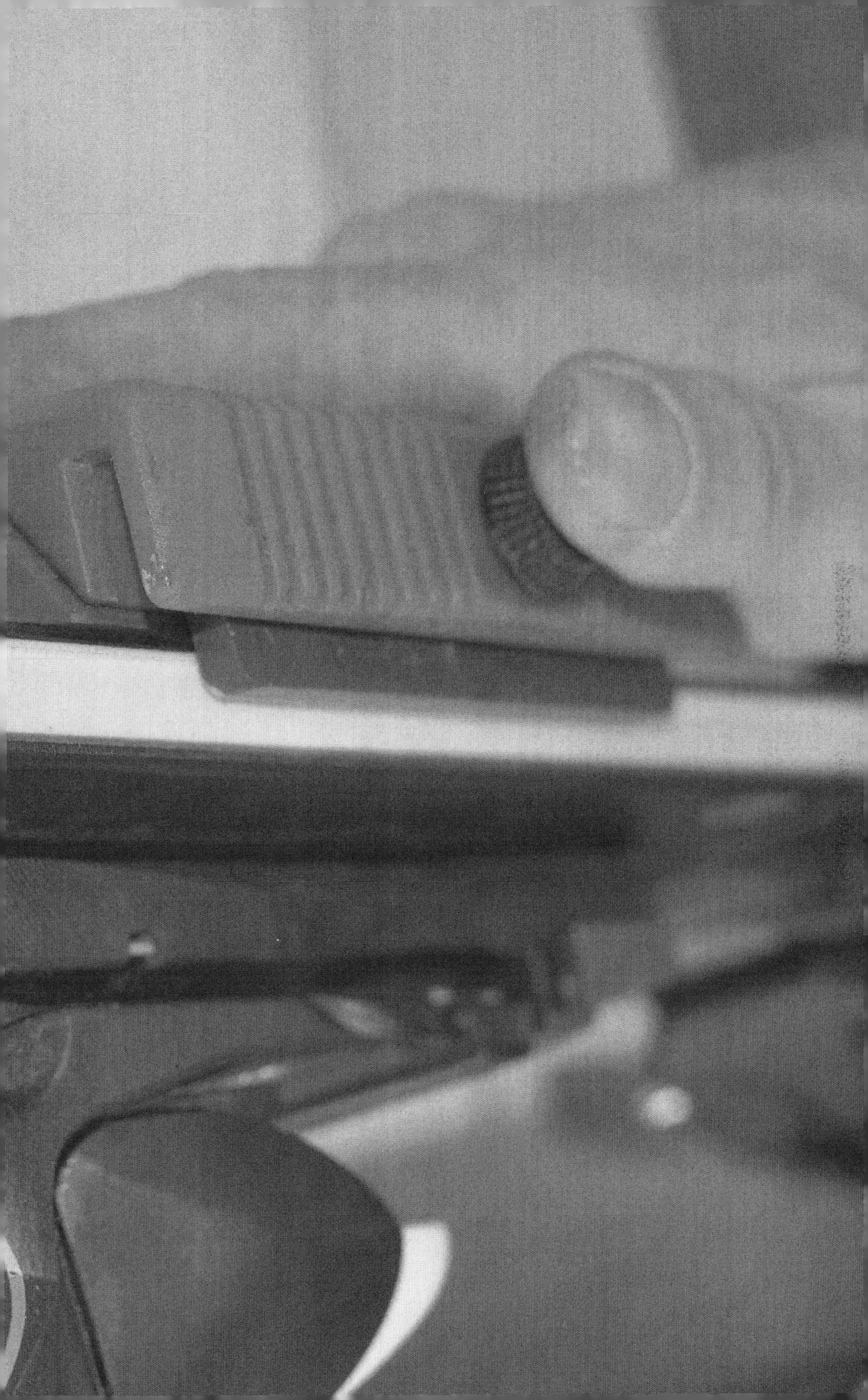

What is bevelling?

The bevel is the angle at which the steel edge of the ski is set. Modifying the bevel can dramatically affect the handling and performance of the ski. There are two sides of the edge to bevel: the base edge and the side edge.

Understanding base edge beveling

A base bevel lifts the edge out of the snow. This makes the ski glide faster, because there is less contact with the snow, but also forces the skier to lean more to find the edge. If the ski does not have enough base bevel, it can dig into the snow and catch the skier off guard. If the ski has too much base bevel, it will become difficult to control. Be careful when first beveling your base edge: if you go over 0.5°, you will not be able to revert to the original angle, because there won't be enough base material. Some common base edge bevels for different ski disciplines are given in the following tables.

Suggested Base Bevel Angles

Ski

Slalom	0–0.5°
GS	0.5–0.75°
Super G	0.75–1.0°
All mountain/expert	0.75–1.0°
All moutain novice/advanced	1.0°

Suggested Base Bevel Angles

Snowboard

Beginner	1.0–2.0°
Intermediate	1.0°
Freerider	1.0°
Spinner	2.0°+
Halfpipe	1.0–2.0° (tip/tail); 0–1.0° (underfoot)
Boardercross	0–1.0°
Slalom	0–0.5°
GS	1.0°

IMPORTANT

These angles are only a rough guide. This is especially true when it comes to ski racing, when the terrain, snow conditions, and athlete all vary. (If you are unsure, check with the manufacturers specifications before making a new bevel.)

Understanding side edge beveling

Side edge bevels normally range from 1–3°: the bigger the bevel, the more the edge will cut into snow (which can be helpful in icy conditions). If the angle of the bevel is too small, the ski will skid and be difficult to control, but if the angle is too great, the edge will cut into the snow so much it will be hard to get off the edge. Some common side edge bevel angles are given in the table below.

Suggested Side Edge Bevel Angles

SKI	
All Mountain Novice	1.0°
All Mountain intermediate	2.0–3.0°
All Mountain Advanced	2.0°
Slalom	3–4°
GS	2–3°
Super G	2–3°

SNOWBOARD

Beginner	0–1.0°
Intermediate	1.0°
Freerider	1.0–2.0°
Spinner	0°
Halfpipe	1.0°
Boardercross	1.0–2.0°
Slalom	2.0–3.0°
GS	2.0°

IMPORTANT

These angles are only a rough guide. This is especially true when it comes to ski racing, when the terrain, snow conditions, and athlete all vary. If you are unsure, check with the manufacturers specifications before making a new bevel.

How to sharpen and tune edges

Sharp edges will allow you to grip the snow, which will help you stay upright instead of sliding down the hill out of control. They also help to prolong the life of your skis, which will you save money in the long term. All in all, keeping your edges sharp can be the difference between having a good or bad day on the slopes.

What you need to sharpen your edges :

- 2x heavy-duty rubber bands
- Ski vice or 2x blocks of wood
- Gummy stone
- Diamond stone
- Base file guide
- Side edge angle guide
- Bastard file (bevelling only)
- Marker pen
- Spray bottle and water

How to sharpen the base edge
(As a rule, it is always better to start with the base edge)

Step 1

Retract brakes: Start by manually pulling the brake up so it is flush with the ski, and then stretch an elastic band from one brake to the other, passing over the heel piece on the binding. This will help keep the brake out of the way while edging your skis.

Step 2

Make sure the skis are clean and the edges are free of wax. Attach the skis to the ski vice with the base facing upwards.

Step 3

Starting with the edge furthest away from you, use the gummy stone to remove any rust or micro burrs.

Step 4

Fix the diamond stone to the base file guide. Set the appropriate bevel if necessary (if unsure, leave it at 0°). Wet the diamond stone using the spray bottle, then slide it over the base edge in smooth, even-pressure strokes that slightly overlap. Do a few full length strokes to help remove any larger burrs. Repeat this process on both edges and both skis.

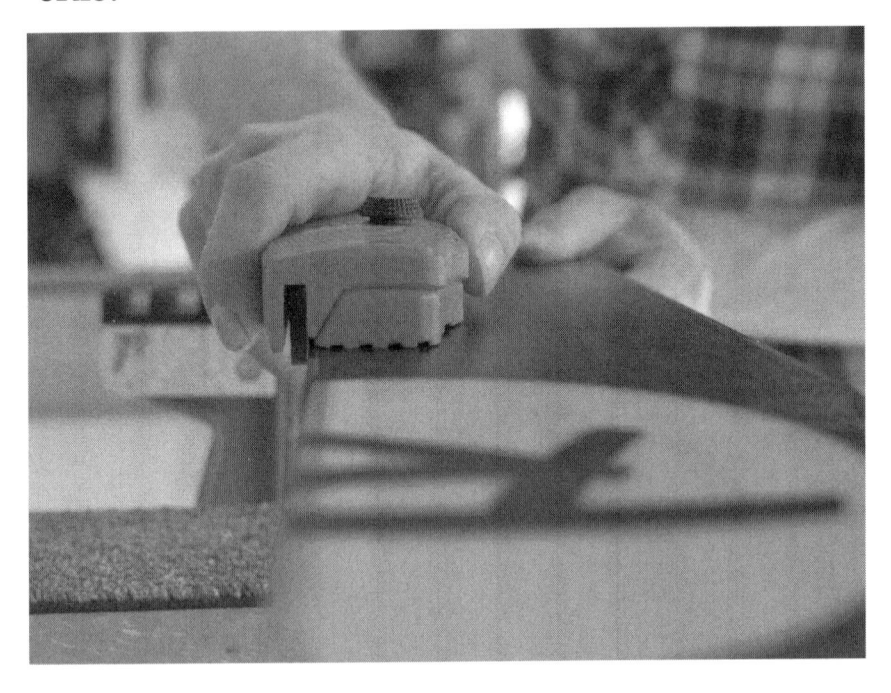

Remember: Only use a diamond stone on your base edge

How to sharpen the side edge

Step 1

Place the skis in the ski vice with the side edge you're working on facing up.

Step 2

Clean the edge with a gummy stone, paying attention to any rust or rock damage.

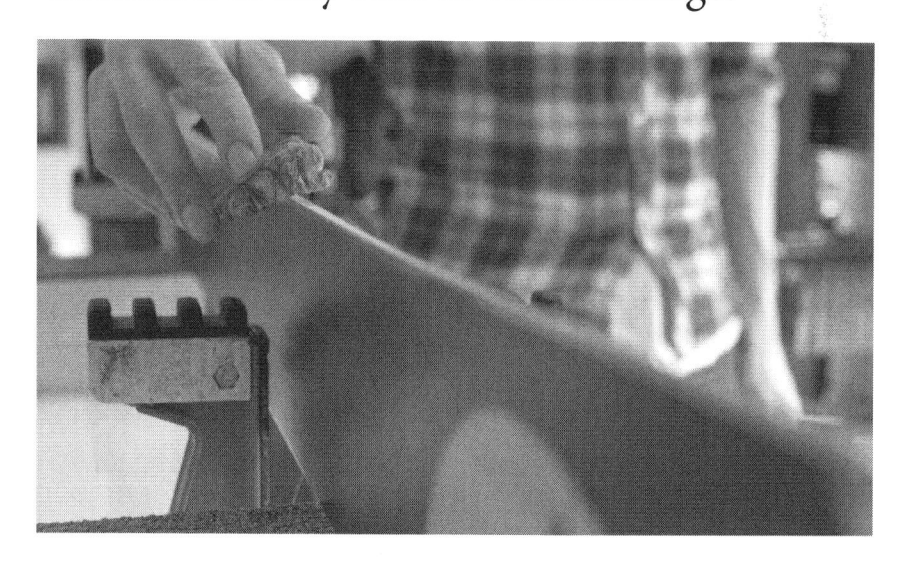

Step 3

Take your marker pen and draw down the whole edge. This will ensure that you don't miss any sections of the edge.

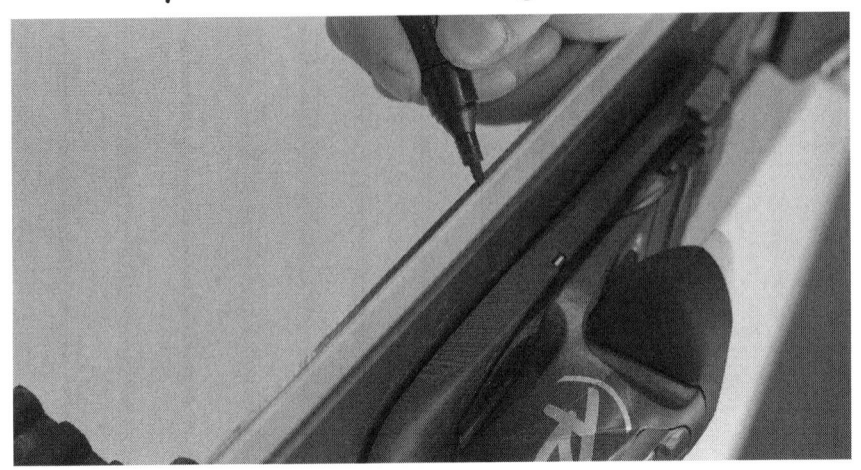

Step 4

If you only want to sharpen the edges, take your file guide, set the appropriate angle, and then insert the diamond stone into the file guide and slide the guide along the edges in long smooth strokes until all the marker pen has been completely scraped off.

Step 5 (Beveling only)

Take your file guide and file, set the desired bevel if required. Start with the edge furthest away and pull the guide towards you around 10-12 times making sure to remove all the marker pen.

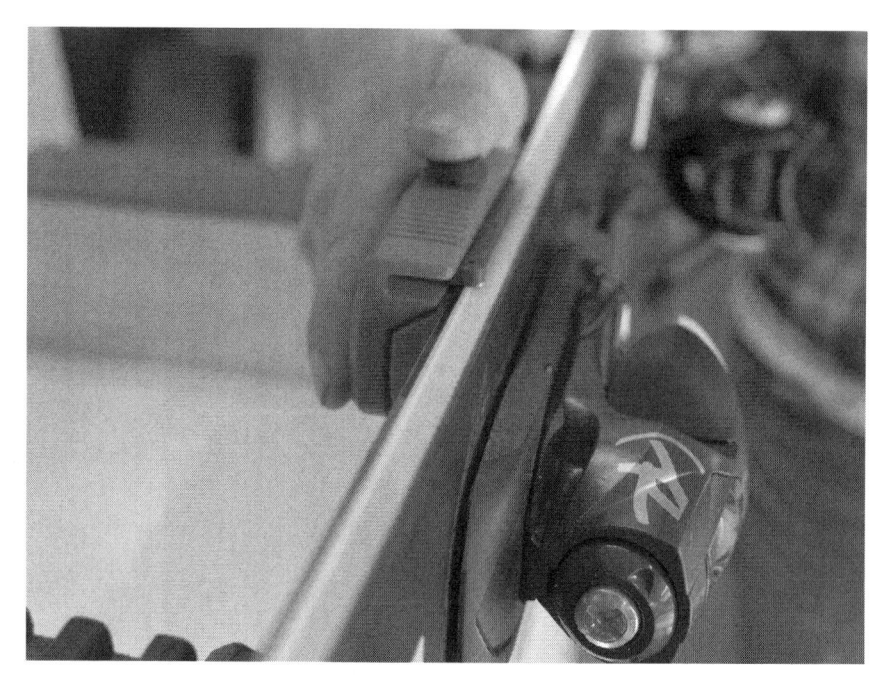

Tip: always use a sharp file, change your file at least once a year.

6

Run the gummy stone at a 45° angle to remove any burrs or serrations left from sharpening your edges. Use the gummy stone lightly: the aim is to clean the edge, not blunt it.

Step 7

It is now necessary to detune the tips and tails. This means dulling, or blunting, the tips and tails to help make turning smoother and less erratic. The area to be detuned extends for around three finger-widths from the point at which the tip/tail starts to curve up (see detuning edges). Taking the gummy stone, rub hard on the area to be detuned until it is blunt (test by scraping your nail on the edge—if none of the nail scrapes off, it is blunt enough).

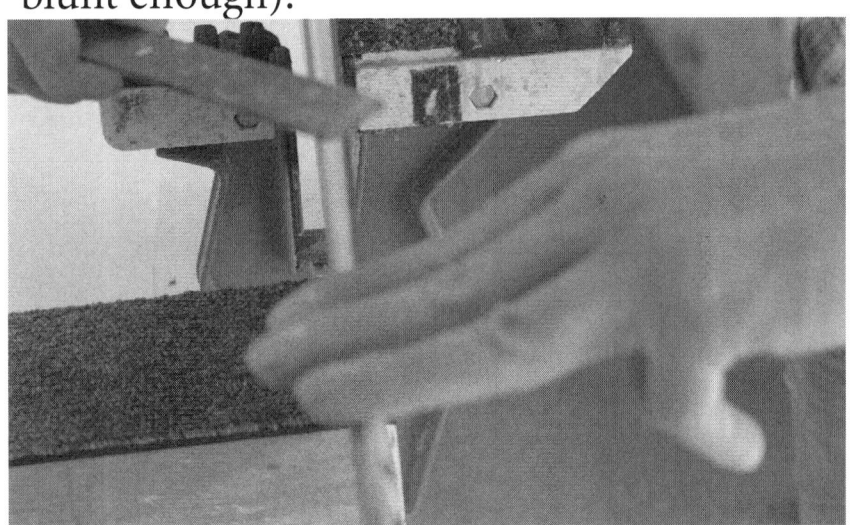

Step 8

Repeat this process on the other edge and on both skis. Apply a layer or two of hot wax (see How to wax skis), then finish by removing the elastic band from the brakes.

Detuning edges

Detuning the edges means to dull (blunt) the tips and tails of skis so that the edges do not initiate the turn to quickly making them grabby. Edges usually will need detuning after they have been sharpened or when bought from new.

How to de-tune skis
Step 1
The rule of thumb is to place three fingers from where the tip and tail of the edge starts to go up. If your skis have a rocker start from where the rocker goes up.

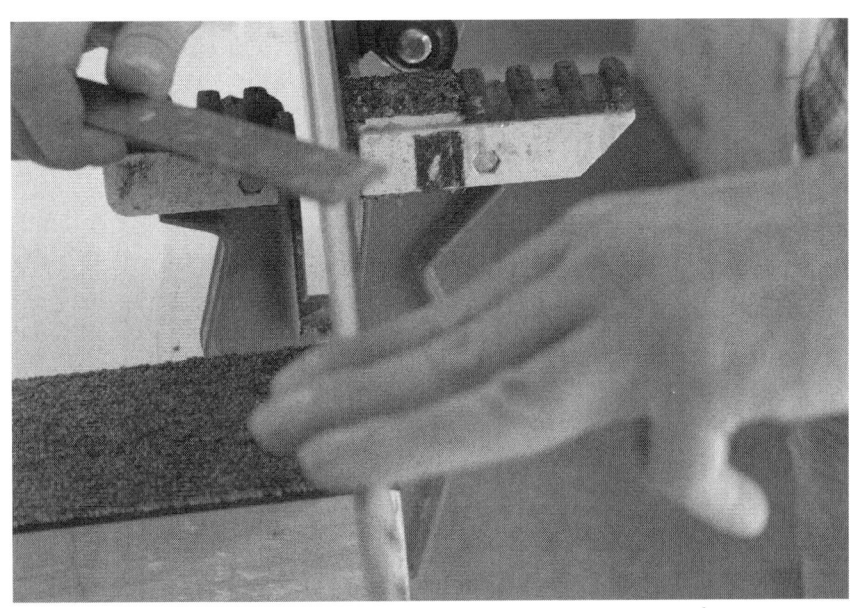

Step 2

Dull off both tips and tails with either a gummy stone or lightly with a file then polished off with gummy stone.

Step 3

Check the edges have been adequately detuned by running your finger nail over the edge, if they do not shave off any nail they have been detuned enough.

Tip: Try experimenting with the amount you detune your edges. This can dramatically affect how the ski will perform for different ski disciplines and snow conditions

Base repairs, fixing scrapes, holes and dings

This section of the book explains how to do base repair. Keeping your ski base in good condition will prolong the life of your skis and help to increase the life span of the ski.

Base repairs, fixing scrapes, holes and dings

No matter whether you ski groomed pistes or hardcore backcountry, you will end up getting scrapes and holes in your skis from time to time. If the scrape does not go through to the core, you can carry on skiing, although your skis will slide more slowly. If the scrape goes through to the core of the ski, you should repair the base as soon as possible, because if water gets into the core your skis may be permanently damaged.

What is P-tex?

P-tex is the name for the polyethylene commonly used to make ski and snowboard bases. P-tex is also used in ski repair to patch holes in skis. It can be bought in candle form, to be lit and then melted into the repair area, and on a roll for use with a special gun, as used by most professional ski shops. When using P-tex, be careful not to drip it onto your skin, because it can cause severe burns.

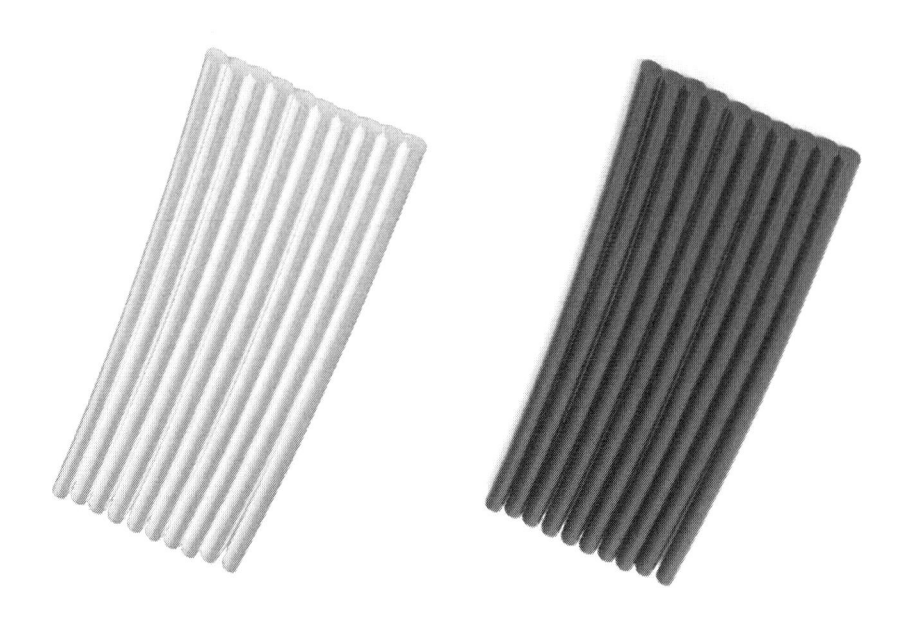

What is metal grip?

Metal grip is an epoxy P-tex mix that is used to repair deep holes (through to the core) or damage next to the edge of the ski. This product should be used to prepare the hole before finishing with a layer of P-tex. Make sure you are in a well-ventilated area when using metal grip, and give it at least an hour to set before applying the P-tex.

How to repair holes in your base

What you will need:
- Metal scraper
- P-tex candle
- Lighter
- Razor blade/scalpel
- Metal brush (optional).

Step 1

Before starting any hole repairs make sure the ski, and especially the damaged area, is dry and not too cold (room temperature). If there is any dampness around the area you plan to fill, and especially for a core shot (a hole that penetrates the base), leave the skis near a heater overnight (but not too close, otherwise the base could melt).

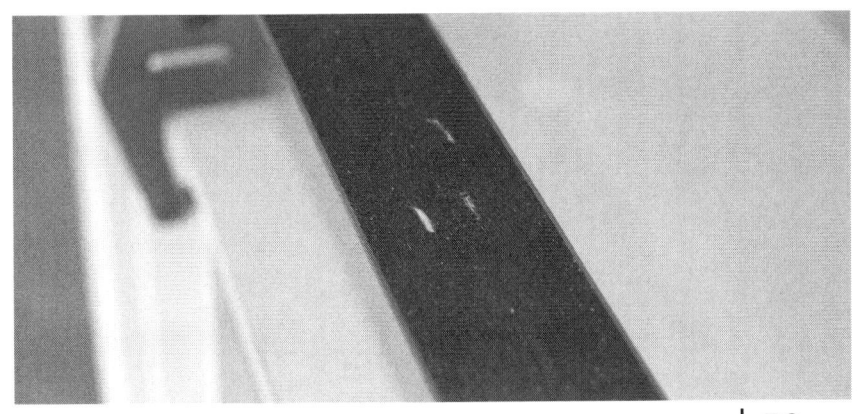

Step 2

Check the problem area for any debris, such as dirt, gravel, or shards of metal, and gently remove with something sharp and pointy—a scalpel is ideal. Next, remove any jagged or protruding bits from around the hole with the metal scraper or a razor blade. It is especially important to remove any excess jagged base when repairing a clear base with clear P-tex—otherwise, the P-tex won't stick and bubbles may appear in the fill.

Step 3

Thoroughly clean the area to be repaired with a base cleaner/de-waxer to ensure the repair bonds well.

Step 4 (Core holes or edge fills only)

Core shots or fills near the edge should be prepared with metal grip to help the P-tex bond. Use a soldering iron or lighter to melt the metal grip into the hole and leave for an hour. For more information, see: https://www.youtube.com/watch?v=tTBuXIpEiIg&t=73

Although metal grip is recommended for deep holes, it is not essential—a well-filled P-tex repair will normally last a fair while.

62 | Base repairs, fixing scrapes, holes and dings

Step 5

Light the P-tex candle and let it drip onto a metal scraper until the flame turns blue and the P-tex starts to runs freely. Hold the candle at about 45° 5–10mm above the repair area, and drip the P-tex into the hole while slowly turning the candle. This should help reduce the amount of carbon build up. Minimizing carbon build up will help the fill to bond more effectively, and result in a cleaner look, especially when using clear P-tex.

Slightly overfill the hole, and then press the metal scraper on top of the repair for about 20 seconds. This pushes the hot P-tex into the repair area. Deeper fills should be filled in 2-3 stages, allowing each fill to cool before applying the next. A word of caution: be extremely careful not to drip any molten P-tex onto your skin or clothes.

Step 6

Once the P-tex has cooled, gently scrape away the excess with a metal scraper or panzer file until the fill is flush with the rest of the base. Pass a sharp plastic scraper over the fill to remove any fine excess. If you have a metal brush, finish by running it over the fill area to help re-structure the base, as this will improve wax absorption. After any repairs, you should always fully wax the skis **(see: How to wax skis)** to help protect the fill.

Waxes and waxing

This section of the book explains how to wax your skis and looks into the different types of waxes available. Keeping your skis waxed is a quick, simple task that will help protect your skis and more importantly make your skis slide well, so you can beat your friends down the mountain.

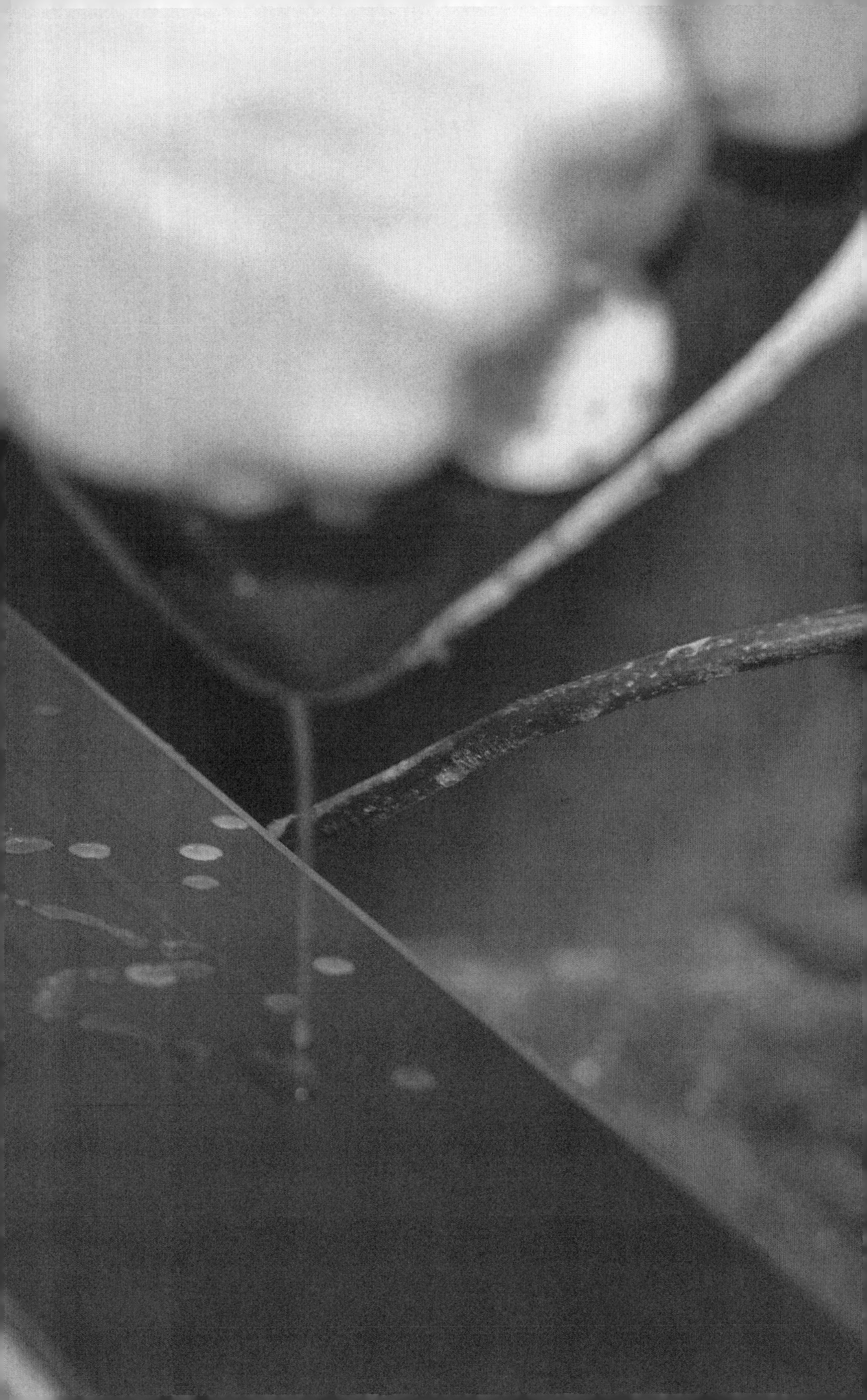

Why do skis need waxing?

For many people, part of the enjoyment of skiing is the sensation of effortlessly gliding around the mountains with their friends. If you start to find it hard to keep up with other people, the solution could be as simple as giving your skis a wax. Ski wax provides two main functions:

1) It acts as a lubricant, allowing your skis to slide better.
2) it helps to protect the skis from oxidation caused by friction, which will eventually decrease their lifespan.

The base of a ski is made from a type of polyethylene, and consists of thousands of tiny holes. These holes act like a sponge, absorbing wax and then expelling it during skiing. As skis pass over the surface of the piste, the temperature and pressure of the ski melts the snow, creating a thin layer of water between the snow and the base of the ski. Water repellent wax works as a lubricant between the base and this layer of water, helping to improve the glide of the ski.

Types of wax

There are three main types of ski wax:

1. **Hydrocarbon waxes:** Every ski should have a base coat of hydrocarbon wax. Recreational skiers will typically use only hydrocarbon wax, whereas ski racers will use this as a base coat.

2. **Fluorocarbon waxes** : Used as an additive after a hydrocarbon wax has been applied, they have better water repellent properties, which makes the skis slide faster. Fluorocarbon waxes are mainly used by ski racers, as they are more expensive and require more preparation.

3. **Graphite additive/Molybdenum (Moly):** In cold dry snow electrostatic builds up and slows the ski down. This graphite additive helps reduce this effect, helping to improve the speed of the ski.

What are temperature waxes?

Temperature waxes are a range of hydrocarbon-based products that are designed to slide faster in specific temperatures. As a rule of thumb, the colder the snow, the harder the wax needs to be to help protect the base of the ski from gripping the coarser snow. The warmer the snow, the softer the wax needs to be to repel the wetter snow.

The color of the wax usually represents the temperatures it should be used for. For example, warm colors like orange, yellow, and pink should be used for warmer snow conditions, and cooler, paler colors like white, purple, and blue should be used for cooler conditions.

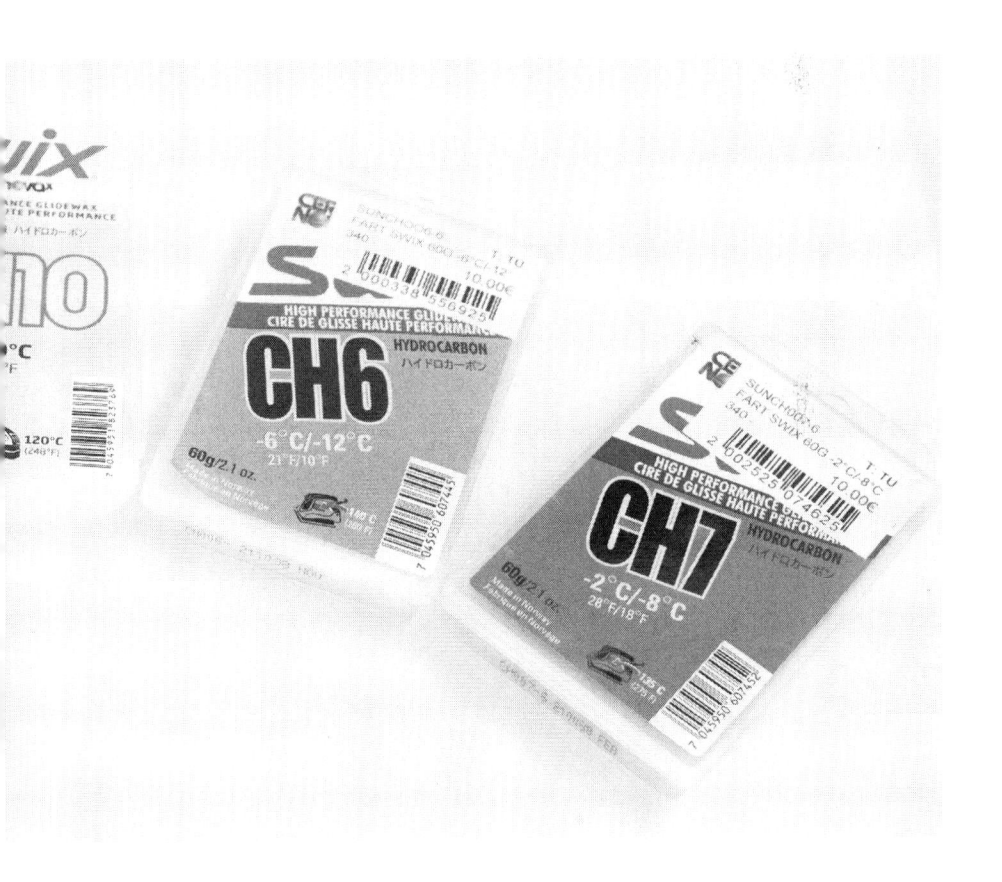

Which type of wax should I use?

Some waxes are suitable for all temperatures (universal), whereas others are temperature-specific.

Universal wax: This is a good wax for most recreational skiers who ski in different temperatures and locations. If you want a 'do it all' wax, this is the one for you.

Temperature-specific waxes: These are for recreational skiers who want to go as fast as possible . Choose the correct wax for the snow conditions, and you will notice a significant improvement in performance over universal wax.

Rub-on wax: This will normally comes with a sponge applicator and can be applied pretty much anywhere. Rub-on wax can be handy to have in your backpack, but only lasts a few runs, so is no substitute for a hot wax.

Fluorocarbon race waxes: These pricey waxes come in powder form and are normally kept purely for racing, as they only last 5–6 runs. If you're looking for the ultimate in wax performance, then apply some fluorocarbon wax after your hydrocarbon wax base coat to give you the winning edge.

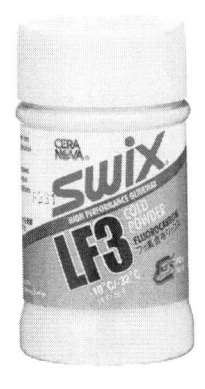

Waxes and waxing | 73

How to wax skis

Before waxing your skis, find a suitable area that is well lit and ventilated. You may also need to lay down plastic sheets to help protect the worktop from the wax. It's also worth wearing some old clothes, because wax is very difficult to remove from clothes and shoes.

What you need to wax skis

- 2x heavy-duty rubber bands
- Ski vice or 2x blocks of wood
- Wax of choice (never use candle wax)
- Iron (a specific wax iron is best, because you can control the temperature for different types of wax. A normal clothes iron will work fine, just don't use water with it)
- Scraper
- Brushes

Step 1

Start by placing your skis on your ski vice or blocks of wood. If your skis have brakes, they will need to be retracted and secured out of the way while waxing your skis. Manually pull the brake up so it is flush with the ski, and then stretch an elastic band from one brake to the other, passing over the heel piece on the binding. This holds the brake out of the way while waxing.

Step 2

Turn you skis over so the base is pointing up, dry the base with a towel, and carefully check the base for any deep holes or scrapes. If you find any, make sure you repair the holes as soon as possible, otherwise water could get into the core and permanently damage your skis (see How to repair holes on page ?). Also remove any debris such as stones or dirt that is caught in the ski. Next, inspect the edges for any cracks or dents. Now is the time to perform any necessary repairs or sharpen the edges (**see**: Base repairs, fixing scrapes, holes and dings).

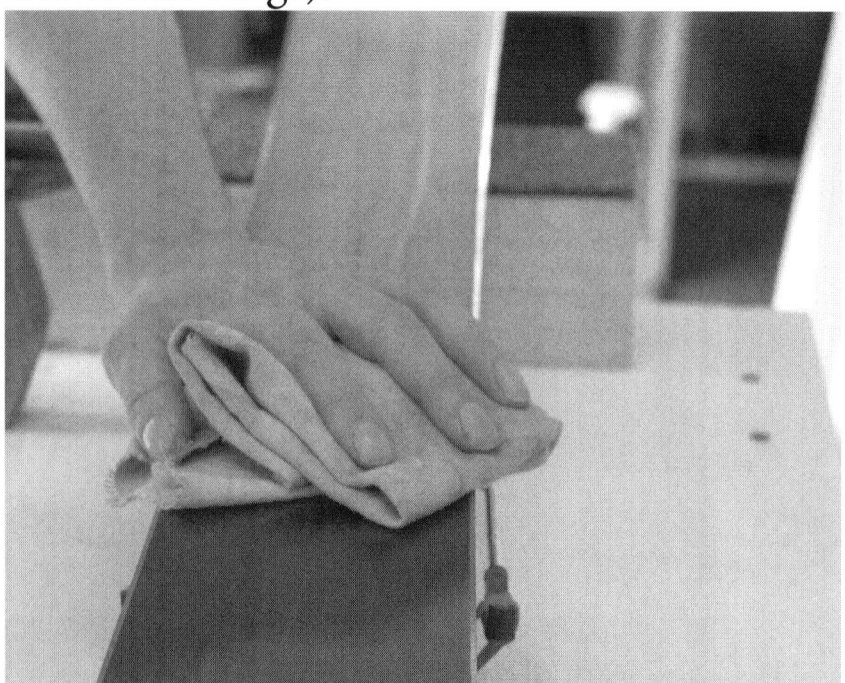

Step 3a

Turn the iron on and set the temperature according to the type of wax: hotter for harder, cold wax and cooler for softer, warm wax. The optimal temperature should be printed on the packet; if in doubt, set the iron so it's hot enough to melt the wax, but not so hot that the wax is smoking.

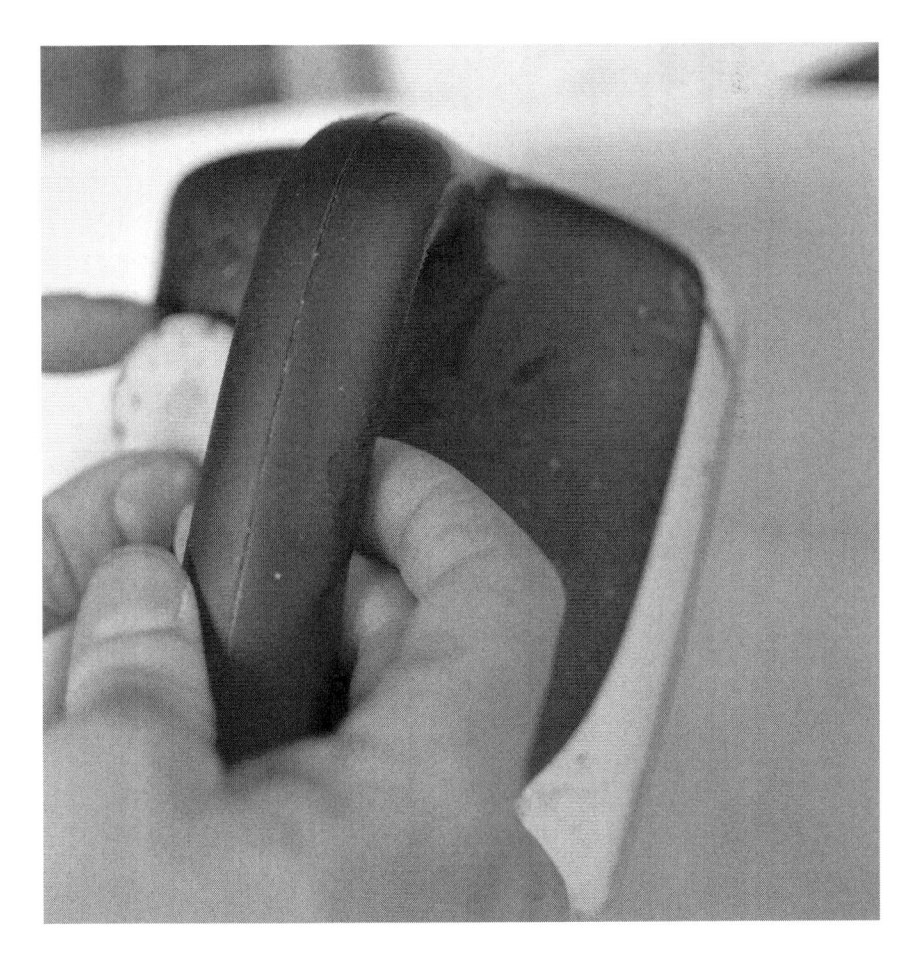

Step 3b

Take the block of wax, and hold it against the iron, about 5–10 cm above the base of the ski. Starting at the tip or tail of the ski, drip molten wax in a zigzag pattern along the length of both skis.

Step 3c

Iron the wax into the base, moving the iron in a circular motion and ensuring that both skis are covered in a coat of wax. Leave the wax to dry for at least 20 minutes to fully soak into the pores of the base. Note: leaving the skisout side in the cold to dry could have the opposite effect and actually push the wax out of the pores. Always finish the waxing process by cleaning your iron with an old rag so it's ready for the next time you wax your skis.

Step 4

First, ensure your plastic (not metal) scraper is sharp (90° edge). This will make scraping easier. Scrapers can be sharpened using a scraper sharpener or a panzer file. Hold the scraper with both hands at around 45° and scrape in long strokes. Keep scraping until all visible wax has been removed. Check for any dry spots (areas of the base that are not shiny from the wax) and, if necessary, repeat steps 3–4.

Step 5

Scraping the edges: Now scrape the excess wax from the edges. Most scrapers have a small notch especially for this purpose. Place the notch on the edge and slide it from tip to tail a few times to make sure all wax has been fully removed from the edges.

Step 6a

Brushing the skis will bring out the texture of the base, resulting in a faster slide. There are many different types of brush for this purpose. If you have a selection of brushes, start with the stiffest and work through to the softest. Unless you are a serious ski racer, a stiff nylon brush will be sufficient. Run the brush from tip to tail around 15 times while applying a moderate amount of pressure.

Step 6b

Then, take a soft brush such as a paintbrush or dustpan brush and remove any excess dust.

Step 7

Finish by removing the rubber bands from your brakes, then sweep up the wax scrapings.

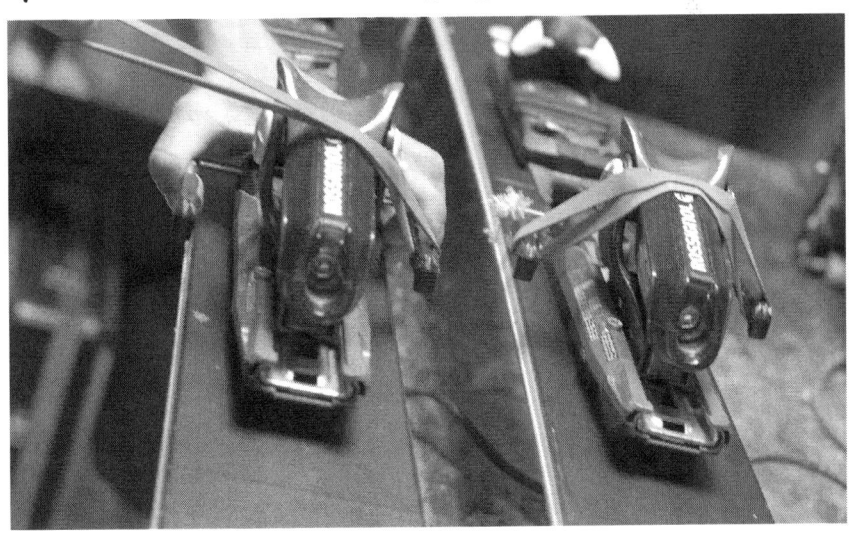

Waxes and waxing

Top tip:

If you want a cheap way of getting a better finish, try using some Scotch-Brite (the green rough side of a washing up sponge). Rub this over the ski quickly to get an amazing shiny, polished finish.

How often do I need to wax my skis?

You cannot wax your skis too often. Waxing your skis makes them water repellent, which allows them to glide faster over the snow. The frequency of waxing will largely depend on the snow conditions and the quality of your skis. If you are regularly skiing on very cold, coarse snow, then you will need to wax your skis more often than if you're skiing on fresh powder.

Dry spots

One of the clearest signs that your base needs a wax is the appearance of oxidation spots. These normally start to occur near the edges. The areas of the skis that still have wax on will be slightly shiny, and any areas that are starting to oxidize will look dull and pale.

Slow coach

If you notice you're going much slower than you typically do, this could also be a sign that it's time to get the waxing iron out.

Do I need to wax new skis?

New skis come with a thin factory wax, which usually dries out after a few runs. Therefore, it's always worth giving new skis at least a couple of coats of hot wax before heading out on the slopes (**see: waxes and waxing**).

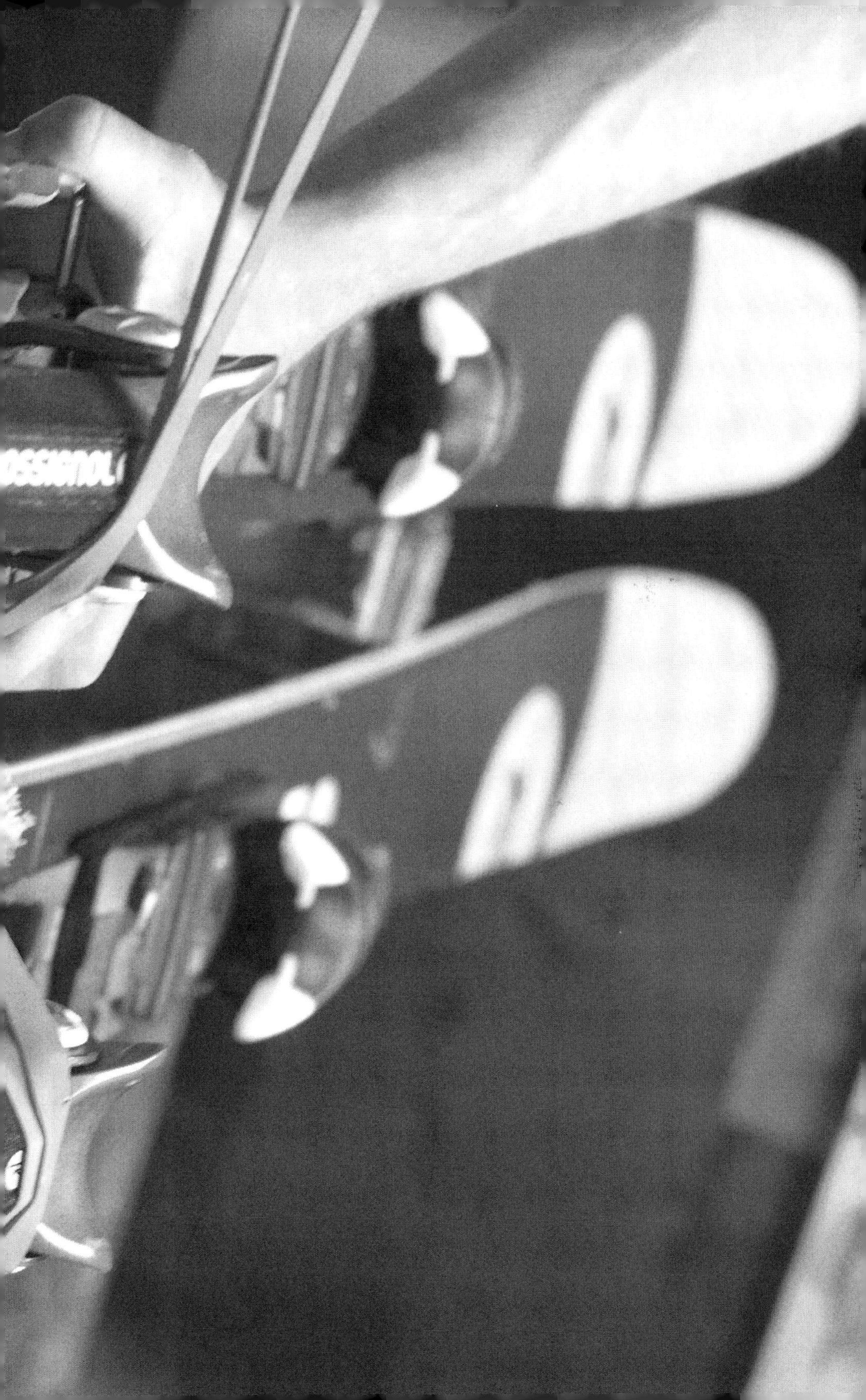
OSSIGNOL

Summer loving

This brief section of the book explains how to take care of your skis during the summer months, so they are ready for action as soon as the snow starts to fall again.

How to protect your skis for the summer

At the end of the winter, it's important to store your skis correctly instead of just throwing them in a bag and leaving them until the following winter. Here are some tips which will help increase the lifespan of your skis, and also save you some money.

Check for damage

Inspect for any damage, starting on the top sheet and side walls. If you find any damage, fill with an epoxy resin, allow to dry overnight, and then lightly sand down with 225-grit sand paper. Next, check the base for any damage, and make repairs where necessary (see: How to repair holes).

Check the edges

Check the edges for any damage such as burrs, dents, or signs of case hardening (a lip of metal on the side edge caused by hard, icy snow or rocks). Next, check whether the edges are sharp by running your finger nail over the edge. If they are sharp, they should shave a thin sliver of nail off. Make any repairs and sharpen the edges if needed (see: How to sharpen and tune edges).

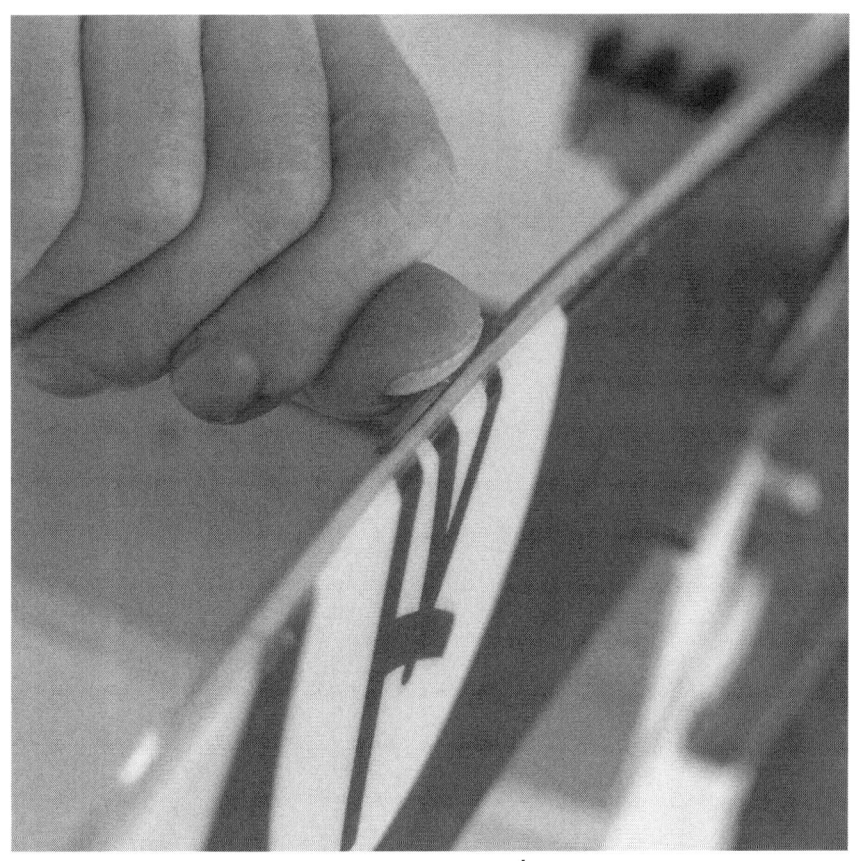

Storage Wax

First, apply a coat of hot wax to help draw out any impurities in the base, and then scape off. Continue this process until the wax comes up clean (**see** waxes and waxing). Apply one last layer of wax, and leave it on (i.e. don't scape it off). This layer of wax helps to protect the skis and edges from oxidation during the summer months.

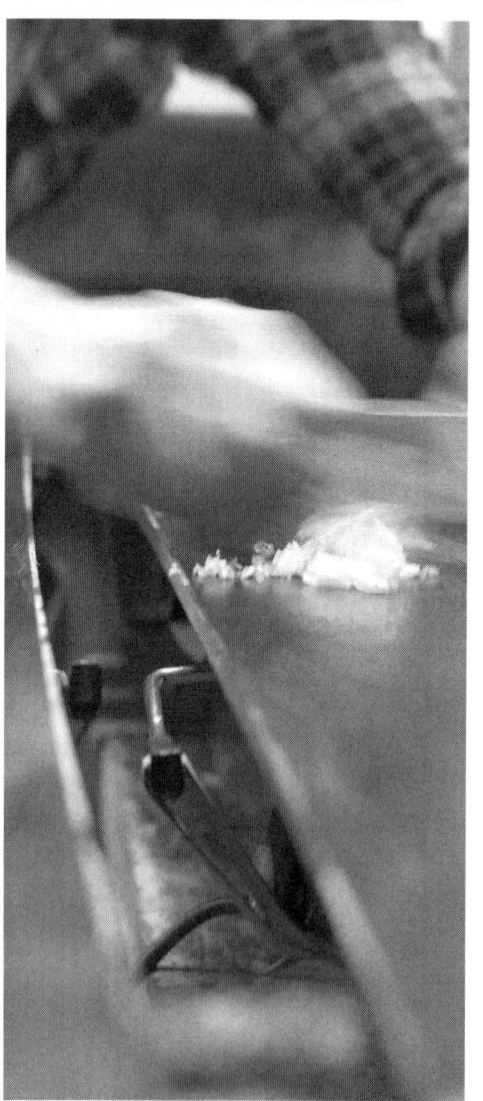

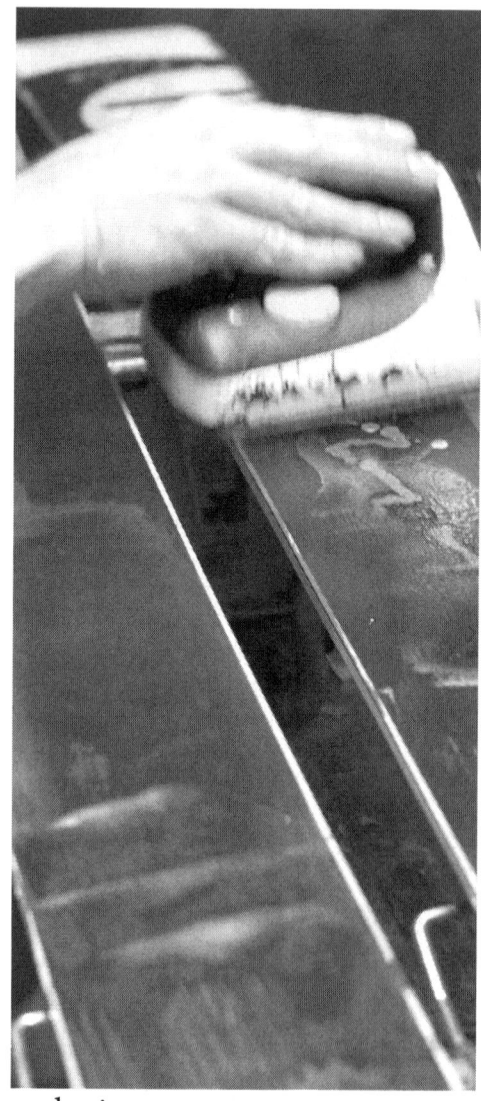

Where to store

Store your skis in a dry place with a consistent temperature, ideally in the house rather than a garage or shed.

Summer loving

INDEX

B

Beveling 4–93, 32–93, 42–93

C

Ceramic stones 16–93
Corks 29–93

D

Detuning 4–93, 14–93, 38–93
Diamond stones 17–93
Dry spots 82–83

E

Edge files 18–93

F

Fluorocarbon 67, 71

G

Graphite additive 67–93
Gummy stones 14–93

M

Metal brushes 25–93
Metal grip 5–93, 56–93, 60–93
Metal scrapers 4–93, 13–93
Molybdenum 67–93
Multiple angle guides 22–93

N

Natural fiber brushes 27–93
Nylon brushes 26–93

O

Oxidation 83

P

Panzer body files 20–93
Plexi-glass scrapers 4–93, 12–93
P-tex 5–93, 13–93, 20–93, 55–93, 56–93, 57–93, 58–93, 60–93, 61–93, 62–93, 63–93

R

Roto-brushes 28–93
Rub-on wax 71–93

S

Scotch-Brite 82–83
Sidewall cutters 4–93, 24–93
Single angle guides 23–93
Ski Irons 10
Ski vices 8–93
Storage Wax 90–91

T

Temperature-specific waxes 70–93
Tune edges 4–93, 41–93, 89–93

U

Universal wax 70–93

W

Waxing
  New skis 84

If you emjoyed reading this book please help a first time author and leave a review on Amazon.com

Printed in Great Britain
by Amazon